Presented To

_____

By

_____

Date

_____

Power Points
FOR DAILY LIVING
Meditation Moments

Dr. Debora F. Grant

HOPE OF VISION PUBLISHING
BRIDGEPORT, CONNECTICUT

Power Points for Daily Living: Meditation Moments
Copyright © 2010 by Dr. Debora F. Grant

All rights reserved. No part of this book may be reproduced, copied, stored or transmitted in any form or by any means – graphic, electronic, or mechanical, including photocopying, recording, or information storage and retrieval systems without the prior written permission of Dr. Debora F. Grant or Hope of Vision Publishing except where permitted by law.

Unless otherwise specified, all Scripture quotations in this book are from The Holy Bible, King James Version. KJV is Public domain in the United States printed in 1987.

Hope of Vision Publishing a division of HOV, LLC.
www.Hopeofvisionpublishing.com
hopeofvision@gmail.com

Cover Design: Kaye Coleman
Cover Image: iStock Photo

Editor: S.O.U.L.E Destiny, LLC

Dr. Debora F. Grant, Sr. Pastor
St. John A.M.E. Church
Columbus, GA 31907
www.drdeboragrant.com

For more information about special discounts for bulk purchases, please contact Dr. Debora Grant at pastordebbie7@aol.com or (706) 442-3244 or visit: www.hopeofvisionpublishing.com or Email: hopeofvision@gmail.com

ISBN 978-0-9831371-1-5
Library of Congress Number: 2010942472

10 9 8 7 6 5 4 3 2 1

Printed in the United States of America

Dedication

I dedicate this book to preserve the legacy of my parents, Joseph J. and Lillie M. Grant, who departed this life only a day apart in November 2009. Their 73 year marriage represents a "Lifetime" of love, and shall forever be an inspiring fragrance in the atmosphere for generations to come.

To my sister Jacquelyn "Jackie" Grant-Collier, a woman of excellence, thank you for always believing in me and supporting me in EVERY facet of my life without fail!

To Rev. Dr. Jeremiah A. Wright, you have been an extraordinary friend and have inspired me throughout my ministerial career. Thank you for keeping it real.

To my girlfriends Detter Willingham, Lynn Spiller, Sharon Davis, Joan Wharton, and Lisa Tait, thank you for knowing me so well and loving unconditionally no matter what! To Peggy Augustine, Linda Jones, and Carolyn Wright, Jeanette Thomas, Georgia Range, my Columbus crew, thank you for your love and support.

I love all of you, and I am eternally grateful for your presence in my life.

Contents

Introduction 9

Power Point #1
    Without Words 11

Power Point #2
    Do You 15

Power Point #3
    The Taste Test 19

Power Point #4
    Somethin Got To Be Did About Dis 23

Power Point #5
    In The Middle 27

Power Point #6
    Success Hurts So Good 31

Power Point #7
    Adona's Eyes 37

30-Day Journal 39

Introduction

Every night at 10:00 p.m. for the past year my girlfriend Dawn DeVeaux reminds me via text message of the enormous power within me. There are nights when I am sleepy and unable to keep my eyes open, but I refuse to rest until I hear the special ring tone indicating I just received a text. Sometimes I have to wait a few moments for the entire message to arrive before opening the text, but it's always well worth the wait! It's like taking a time-release power capsule before going to bed. It works on me through the night and gives me strength for the day to come. So far, I have received over 300 capsules (messages) of empowerment from Dawn. No matter what's going on in my world, at 10:00 p.m., I stop to read her text, and then I take a moment to reflect and pray.

Dawn sent me a wonderful quote from Barbara Harris, the first African-American female Bishop in the Episcopal Church. The message said, "Honor yourself, the truth of who you are. In so doing, develop yourself fully, mind, body and spirit. Always offer your service without measure. It will fill you up." Wow, this is a powerful point to end my day and empower me to begin a new one. I wish everyone had a sista-girlfriend like Dawn!

I pray this book of messages will motivate you just as I am inspired nightly by my friend Dawn. In addition to my daily enlightenment, my sister Jackie has encouraged me all of my life. I pray these Power Points will give you strength for living a powerful life everyday of your life.

Get powered up and you will have what you need to help empower others!

Power Point #1
WITHOUT WORDS

The joy of the Lord is my strength.
~Nehemiah 8:10~

Words are powerful, but there are moments when complete silence conveys more than any carefully crafted words.

I'll tell you a story about a pastor who went to see one of his members who stopped coming to church. When he arrived and knocked on the door, she opened it and welcomed him in. They went into the living room and sat in front of the fireplace. Having not spoken a word beyond their greetings he reached into the fireplace and pulled out an ember and placed it on the outer hearth. As they sat there in silence for a little while, the ember started to lose its glow. Just as it went out, the pastor stood up and said, "It's time for me to go." He picked up the iron poker and placed the piece of burnt wood back into the fireplace and watched it light up again.

The lesson he conveyed, "without words," was when you're out of the church too long, eventually, you will lose your glow.

Maybe you were hurt, experienced an unkind act, or maybe you were a victim of malicious gossip. As a result, you started to withdraw from those people who disappointed you, and the place where you were disappointed. The church is the very place where God wants you to be. You become cynical and judgmental and lose the fire you once had. Today is the day you must declare the devil to be a liar and speak deliverance and healing into your life.

Beloved, don't allow anything or anyone to steal your joy for the Lord. Don't allow the disappointments and the distractions to derail your destiny. Don't allow headaches and heartbreaks to hinder your healing. Don't allow the mess and the mistreatment to minimize your worth and

most of all, don't allow the problems and the pretenders to postpone your praise. God wants to be close to you and God wants to be the fuel for your fire. Don't lose your glow!

Go ahead and get back into the fire.

Pray with me: God it seems my attitude as a result of my disappointments interferes with my getting closer to you and prevents me from celebrating the joy that comes only from knowing you. Please give me faith and strength to let go of the past, so I may honor you with all my heart, with all my soul, and with all mind. Amen.

A Moment of Empowerment

True joy is not obtained the world's way, it comes from the Lord! The world's joy is based upon positions, possession, and power; all of which are temporal. The joy that comes from the Lord is rooted in His presence and promise! When true joy comes, you must be determined to grab it and not let it go easily.

I've allowed these things to interfere with my joy:

_____

_____

_____

_____

_____

_____

_____

Power Points for Daily Living: Meditation Moments

Release them and repeat these words:

God I surrender those things I have allowed to interfere with my joy. Take it away from me. In the Name of Jesus, I pray. Amen.

Now that you have released those obstacles, think about things that bring you joy and list them below.

I get joy when I:

_____

_____

_____

_____

_____

_____

_____

_____

_____

_____

_____

_____

_____

_____

_____

_____

Power Points for Daily Living: Meditation Moments

Embrace the things that give you joy and pray this prayer:

PRAYER OF EMPOWERMENT

Lord, I thank you for my strength which comes from your joy. You have given me something the world cannot take from me. Hallelujah! I am empowered to be my best self and to give my best to you no matter what obstacles come my way. In the Name of Jesus, I pray. Amen.

Power Point #2
DO YOU!

I can do all things through Christ who strengthens me.
~Philippians 4:13~

Listen to this Power Point, "Do not allow the things you cannot do interfere with the things you can do." These are the words of former UCLA coach John Wooden. You can build your life around this truth. Too often we focus on wrong things, the negative instead of the positive, the failures instead of the successes, and the bad times instead of the good times. Then we become puppets to our short falls and operate on our limitations instead of our abilities. When asked to perform a specific task that we think we are incapable of, we often do absolutely nothing. What a waste! When you find yourself in those situations, think of it as an opportunity to do what you can and give what you're capable of giving…YOUR BEST!

God has given us a special gift and blessed us with our portion so we are positioned to be a blessing.

Take a moment to discover what you do well and do it! All of us have limitations; however, we should not define ourselves by them. The Word of God reminds us that we are many members, with different functions, representing one body. What an awesome image! Many of us have been given the gift to teach, nurture, or encourage, while others motivate, comfort, and pray. Whatever your gift is, get excited about yourself and all that you have to offer and "do you!" Whenever the opportunity presents itself for you to use your gifts, use these moments to reveal what God has done in your life.

Don't allow the things you cannot do keep you from doing the things you can do for God, for self, and for others. I always say, "Little becomes a lot when you place it in the Master's hand."

Lean in closer, I want to whisper something to you—because you feel you

can't, don't discourage others who can.

Pray with me: Thank you Lord for blessing me. Teach me how to use my blessings wisely according to your will, so I will use every opportunity to please you. In the Name of Jesus, I pray. Amen.

A Moment of Empowerment

Often times, we don't do because we don't know what we do best! We become enslaved by the things we cannot do and we don't explore the things we can do. Ask yourself this question, "Am I a hostage to my shortcomings?"

List several things you cannot do:

_____
_____
_____
_____
_____
_____
_____
_____
_____
_____
_____
_____

Power Points for Daily Living: Meditation Moments

Release them and repeat these words:

God I surrender those things that have kept me from using my gift for your glory. Take it away from me. In the Name of Jesus, I pray. Amen.

Now that you have released those barriers, think about those things that make you uniquely you! The abilities you possess that will allow you to "DO YOU!"

List several things you can do:

_____

_____

_____

_____

_____

_____

_____

_____

_____

_____

_____

_____

_____

_____

Power Points for Daily Living: Meditation Moments

Embrace the things you believe you can do and pray this prayer:

PRAYER OF EMPOWERMENT

Lord I thank you for gifting me with my special gifts. I will honor you by utilizing my strength to make each day count. I will not succumb to the things I cannot do. I will do the things that you have empowered me to do. In the Name of Jesus, I pray. Amen.

Power Point #3

THE TASTE TEST

O taste and see that the Lord is good.
~Psalm 34:8~

The proof is in the pudding! I know you've heard this saying before haven't you? One day I tried it, and you know what, the proof was in the pudding. I discovered that I did not like the taste of the pudding.

I enjoy great food and entertaining. From time to time, I will invite friends over to experience great fun and great food. Several of my friends are chefs and they each will prepare one of their signature dishes. My friends and I would gather to try new recipes and some old favorites. Without identifying who made what dish, we would display the creations on the table, stand back, and let the tasting begin. We'd listen to the sound of pleasure to determine which dish passed the taste test!

Then each of the chefs would brag about the many ingredients, the food prep, and the time it took to bake, grill, fry, broil, or stew. It never failed, every time they recaptured the efforts they put into their succulent creation, they always held back that SPECIAL ingredient.

I'm not the greatest chef, but I have a great recipe handed down from my parents that I want to share with you. This recipe has a very special ingredient, and I promise not to keep it from you. I extend a special invitation for you to "taste and see that the LORD is good."

Many have had experiences of the past that left a bitter taste and find it hard to get rid of the bitterness. Every time you go back in the recesses of your mind, the thought of it causes you to regurgitate the same actions or reactions. God wants to sweeten your life's experience. Don't be consumed by the bitter dish of the past. Taste and see that the Lord is good! Every ingredient you need to experience the goodness of God is available to you, including that special ingredient which is GOD'S LOVE.

Everything God serves to us is blended with God's unconditional love for us!

God's goodness cannot simply be confined within the occasional struggles or the difficult battles we fight from time to time. In fact, God's goodness is defined by every moment that we experience God's grace, mercy, forgiveness, and presence. In others words, to CONFINE God's goodness implies that God is good only when good things happen. The reality is, God is always good! When you go through the challenges of life, go ahead, taste and see how good God is.

Jackie Gleason, a comedian and actor from the 70's, made popular the phrase "How sweet it is!" It reminded the viewing audience weekly no matter what situation you find yourself in, life is sweet. With that thought in mind, I say to you, "How sweet it is" to be loved by God unconditionally every day of your life.

Just taste and see, because the proof IS in the pudding!

A Moment of Empowerment

God is as good as you need God to be! It simply means that God's goodness to you is designed especially for you! Good can only get better if you are opened to it!

List several things that left a bad taste in your spirit:

___

___

___

___

___

___

___

Power Points for Daily Living: Meditation Moments

Release them and repeat these words:

God I surrender all the bitterness that has kept me from enjoying my life in Christ. Take it away from me. In the precious Name of Jesus, I pray. Amen.

Now that you have torn down this wall, think about God's goodness in your life.

List some of God's goodness:

_____

_____

_____

_____

_____

_____

_____

_____

_____

_____

_____

_____

_____

_____

_____

Power Points for Daily Living: Meditation Moments

Embrace God's goodness and pray this prayer:

PRAYER OF EMPOWERMENT

Lord I thank you for your goodness and your faithfulness towards me. I will honor you with a steadfast love and an unwavering faith so my life will be sweeter as I come to know you better. I am empowered by your goodness! Amen.

Power Point #4
"Somethin Got to be Did About Dis!"

The devil comes to steal, kill and destroy.
~John 10:10~

My girlfriend Linda told me a story of the dilemma of a little old woman who had very little education. This woman religiously made payments on furniture she placed on lay-a-way at a downtown store in her community. When she made her final payment, the furniture was delivered to her home. After it was unloaded and placed in her room, she discovered it was defected. Feeling a little frustrated, she went back to the store and spoke with the manager. After filing her complaint, they refused to refund her and even worse, they refused to take it back. Outraged, she went to the trusted community attorney. After she told him what happened; she abruptly stood to her feet, slammed her purse on the desk, placed her hands on her hips and with a stern voice she said, "Somethin got to be did about dis!"

Have you ever been fed up with the lies, confusion, corruption, and deception? Have you ever felt used, abused, unappreciated, humiliated, devalued, or dehumanized? If the answer is yes, these are the moments in life where you must put your foot down, take a stand, and declare, "Somethin got to be did about dis!" This is not the time to be grammatically correct, proper, polite, or pleasing! Take authority in your life while trusting in God for guidance and direction. That's right, take authority because the enemy will try to render you hopeless and powerless. He will trick you, confuse you, cheat you, and cause you to doubt what you know. If that's not enough, he will steal from you, kill, and destroy you. Whether or not you want to accept it we are in the midst of a spiritual warfare! It's time for you to declare, "No weapon formed against you will prosper." You must have enough faith in God to know that God is able to do all things and will be your refuge and your strength in times of trouble. Just as the old woman marched into the lawyer's

office, trusting him to handle her business, you must go to God and trust Him with your business.

When you see the enemy coming, trying to trip you up, set you off, beat you down, take you out, or work you over, go to God in prayer and declare, "Somethin got to be did about dis."

Pray with me: Dear God, give me the courage to face my enemy each day with complete trust that you are with me all the way. When things become too much for me to handle, give me the wisdom to come to you. In the Name of Jesus, I pray. Amen.

A Moment of Empowerment

One of the most defining moments in life is when you declare with clarity "Enough is enough!" I will no longer be a victim of my circumstances because I am more than a conqueror and the enemy will not reign victorious in my life. It's time to take authority!

List a few circumstances where the enemy tried to destroy you:

_____
_____
_____
_____
_____
_____
_____
_____
_____

Release them and repeat these words:

Nothing will entangle me in a web of defeat. I claim victory in my family, on my job, in my home, over my finances, and in every area of my life. I release the strongholds in the Name of Jesus, Amen.

Now that you have taken authority in your life, what are some things that you refuse to let the devil have:

I refuse to let the devil have:

_____

_____

_____

_____

_____

_____

_____

_____

_____

_____

_____

_____

_____

_____

Power Points for Daily Living: Meditation Moments

Embrace them and pray this prayer:

PRAYER OF EMPOWERMENT

God I thank you for the victory over my enemy in every circumstance of my life, in the Name of Jesus, I pray. Amen.

___

___

___

___

___

___

___

___

___

___

___

___

___

___

Power Point #5

IN THE MIDDLE

*For I know the plans I have for you says the Lord,
plans to prosper you and not to destroy you.
~Jeremiah 29:1~*

Don't stop in the middle and don't quit. I know you've been told this a million times throughout your life's journey. No matter how many times we hear it, there's always one more river to cross, one more mountain to move, and one more cross to carry and it all seems undoable. If you stop in the middle, you will be stuck in the misery of the moment. You will drown in the river of life, tumble down the rough side of the mountain and the cross you're carrying will become a heavier load. That's what will happen if you stop right now.

You know what? You've got to keep moving because God has something greater for you on the other side. Believe me! You must have complete Trust in God. The Word of God tells us in Jeremiah 29:11, "For I know the plans I have for you says the Lord, plans to prosper you and not to destroy you." It's a wonderful truth to know that God has already mapped out a main plan for each of us. I have often heard people say that while we are trying to figure it out, God has already worked it out!

If you stop in the middle, oh well, there goes the plan. If you want to quit anything, quit smoking, quit lying to yourself, quit settling for less, quit blaming others for your life's choices, quit making excuses, but never quit on your future.

Allow me to share an experience with you. I was driving in a storm one day trying to make my way back home. The rain was so heavy I could not see the road ahead clearly. Driving slowly down the highway, I saw many cars pull to the side of the road. As I passed by, I thought to myself maybe I should pull over. However, the Holy Spirit said, "Keep moving." Through the rain, lightening, and thunder I kept moving and the rain started to ease up and eventually it stopped. Wow, I made it! I looked back in my rearview mirror and could see the down pour that looked like a solid gray wall and I remembered thinking, look what God has brought me through. Had I stopped in the middle, I would have remained in the storm.

Beloved, don't stop in the middle of your storm. Keep moving until you come out of the storm. There is a blessing beyond your trials and tribulations with your name on it. I'll say it again, "DON'T QUIT," because what God has for you cannot be attained in the middle.

Pray with me: Thank you God for looking out for my future and for giving me the victory beyond the middle, Amen.

A Moment of Empowerment

My future has more power than my past and more potential than my present. I WILL NOT QUIT!

List those things that you abandoned "In the middle":

_____

_____

_____

_____

_____

_____

_____

_____

_____

Power Points for Daily Living: Meditation Moments

Release them and repeat these words:

God you are the author and finisher of my life. You have shaved me of my past, sustained me in my present, and secured my future. Anything that comes against your plan for my life, take it away from me, in the precious Name of Jesus, I pray. Amen.

Now that you have torn down another barrier, take this moment to envision your future.

What vision do you have for your future?

_____
_____
_____
_____
_____
_____
_____
_____
_____
_____
_____
_____
_____
_____
_____

Embrace them and pray this prayer:

PRAYER OF EMPOWERMENT

God you have always been the way, the truth and the light and I thank you and praise you for better things to come in my future. In the Name of Jesus, I pray. Amen.

___

___

___

___

___

___

___

___

___

___

___

___

___

___

___

Power Point #6
SUCCESS HURTS SO GOOD!

Let us not be weary in well doing: for in due season we shall reap.
~Galatians 6:9~

We have often heard the saying, "No Pain, No Gain." It's true; if your vision is worth attaining then it's going to take some straining. That is how I say it!

The road to success is not paved with miles and miles of successes. You will encounter pot holes, curves, detours, bumps, and a few speed breakers along the way. From time to time you might witness or become involved in a few crashes on the journey.

When we see people who have achieved a level of success, we assume things have always been good for them; however, there is always a story of overcoming behind the story of success. They didn't just wake up to success; there were occasional struggles along the way. We don't always see the tears, sweat, jealousy, setbacks and set ups. What we see is the finished product and not the fight and the faith process!

While there is no secret to what God can do, there are certainly some things that are hidden from our view. To get to the Gods unseen plan for us, we must push through the pain. I put it this way, "In order to get to it, we have to push through it!"

The pain that comes in your struggle towards success is enough to make you want to holla and throw up both your hands in surrender. However, in the face of your struggles, when you throw up your hands, do it to surrender to God's purpose and plan for your life. Trust God completely as your navigation system on the road to your success.

The word of God reminds us not to be weary in well doing because in **due season** we shall reap the harvest, if we don't give up or give in.

So…enjoy the pain!!!

Your success will cause:
- Your faith to be challenged
- Your fears to be heightened
- Your focus to be distracted

But it will also cause:
- Your heart to be awakened
- Your creativity to be released
- Your character to be developed
- Your destiny to be fulfilled
- Future generations to be influenced

Your success is something worth waiting for, fighting for, and going for!

Find ways to:
- Turn your setbacks into setups
- Your stumbling blocks into stepping stones
- Your sufferings into strength

Don't allow the struggles you are facing right now keep you from achieving success. SUCCESS is not without a struggle.

Let's pray: God you brought Joseph from the pit to the palace, the Israelites from slavery to freedom, and Jesus from persecution to resurrection. You are behind every successful story and I trust you completely with my success. Just as you did it for them I know you will do it for me! Now my faith looks up to you Oh God, for guidance, wisdom and strength. In the name of Jesus, I pray. Amen.

Power Points for Daily Living: Meditation Moments

A Moment of Empowerment

Today I celebrate every moment of pain in my life. My success stands firm because of it. Whatever it takes to be all that God has created me to be, I'm in it to win it!

Write down things you feel you were a failure in:

_____
_____
_____
_____
_____
_____
_____
_____
_____
_____
_____
_____
_____
_____
_____
_____
_____

Release them and repeat these words:

My failures are opportunities to flourish and become more faithful and fruitful!

Now that you have reflected on your failures, refuse to give them power and release them! Allow the pains of the past to become power behind your passion to overcome.

Now list things you must overcome to succeed:

_____

_____

_____

_____

_____

_____

_____

_____

_____

_____

_____

_____

_____

_____

Power Points for Daily Living: Meditation Moments

Embrace them and pray this prayer:

PRAYER OF EMPOWERMENT

God, I thank you that all things work together for the good of those who love you! I praise you for using my hurts as my help. In the Name of Jesus, I pray. Amen.

Power Points for Daily Living: Meditation Moments

Power Point #7

ADONA'S EYES

Several years ago I was hanging out with my 5-year-old great niece. After a day of shopping and eating out at Benihana, one of her favorite restaurants, we were on our way to my house. As I approached the house, pulled into the driveway and pressed the button to open my garage door, Adona made an astonishing statement. She said, "Auntie, you need to get a big house like my Auntie Patrice." I responded, "Adona, I have seven bedrooms, five and a half bathrooms, two kitchens, two family rooms, a large office, living room, breakfast room, and a formal dining room, baby my house is BIG." She then made this powerful observation, "Well Auntie, I'm just a little girl, and I only have little eyes, and I can only see little things!"

What an amazing truth! Some people have little eyes and can only see little things. They are the ones in your life that will never celebrate your accomplishments, dreams and aspirations. They always think of obstacles and reasons why you should not reach for something greater or better.

Everyone cannot handle the best part of you! Their view may not always encompass all God has in store for you. Seeing little things with the eyes of a little girl, is ok for little girls, but it is not ok for one who is mature. Why waste your time or their time showing big things to people with little ability to see them. Oops, did I step on your toes?

Let me give you a word of advice, blindfold ALL 'little eye' people you know, put them behind you, with their hands on your shoulder and lead them to what you see!

Finally, as a little girl, whenever I put more food on my plate than I could eat, my mother would say, "Your eyes are too big." TRUE, my eyes were much bigger than my little stomach. What a mess! However, as a child of God, our eyes are just the right size for us to see what God wants us to see, if we are receptive. So if you have big eyes, don't allow anyone to limit what you see. Go for it! Achieve it! For with God all things are possible.

Pray with me: Lord I thank you for eyes that are just the right size for me to see and achieve greater and better things. I believe it and I receive it, in the Name of Jesus, I pray. Amen.

A Moment of Empowerment

I SEE greater possibilities in my future and my future begins today!

What is one BIG thing that you believe God for?

_____

_____

_____

Envision that one thing and Embrace it as though it exist now. Pray this prayer:

Prayer of Empowerment

I receive every great and wonderful blessing you have for my life! I will not be limited by the small eyes of others. I speak greatness over my life. In the Name of Jesus, I pray. Amen.

_____

_____

_____

Power Up! This Is Your Story

For the next 30 days listen for God's clear voice
and discover your own Power Points.

Power Points for Daily Living: Meditation Moments

30~Day
Journal Pages

Power Points for Daily Living: Meditation Moments

DAY 1
A Day for Miracles

A miracle is something inside you
Marianne Williamson

Power Points for Daily Living: Meditation Moments

Power Points for Daily Living: Meditation Moments

DAY 2
Worship

What is so critical is that we worship regularly and have fellowship as we seek after the peace that only God can give.
Iyanla Vanzant

Power Points for Daily Living: Meditation Moments

Power Points for Daily Living: Meditation Moments

DAY 3
Choose to live!

When you die to the past, you live in the present and have hope for the future!

Power Points for Daily Living: Meditation Moments

Power Points for Daily Living: Meditation Moments

DAY 4
PUSH today!

<u>P</u>ray <u>U</u>ntil <u>S</u>omething <u>H</u>appens.

Power Points for Daily Living: Meditation Moments

Power Points for Daily Living: Meditation Moments

DAY 5
Win today!

Winning is not an option, it's the only choice!

_____
_____
_____
_____
_____
_____
_____
_____
_____
_____
_____
_____
_____
_____
_____
_____
_____
_____
_____
_____

Power Points for Daily Living: Meditation Moments

Power Points for Daily Living: Meditation Moments

DAY 6
LOL!

You are blessed so let the world know it. LIVE OUT LOUD!

Power Points for Daily Living: Meditation Moments

Power Points for Daily Living: Meditation Moments

DAY 7
Face It!

In order to fix anything, you must be willing to face it.

Power Points for Daily Living: Meditation Moments

Power Points for Daily Living: Meditation Moments

DAY 8
Go Wireless!

Pray!

Power Points for Daily Living: Meditation Moments

Power Points for Daily Living: Meditation Moments

DAY 9
Sit this one out!

The Lord will fight for you; you need only to be still
Exodus 14:14 (NIV)

Power Points for Daily Living: Meditation Moments

Power Points for Daily Living: Meditation Moments

DAY 10
Laugh Out Loud!

*He will yet fill your mouth with laughter
and your lips with shouts of joy.*
Job 8:21 (NIV)

Power Points for Daily Living: Meditation Moments

Power Points for Daily Living: Meditation Moments

DAY 11
Get Closer!

Draw near to God and he will draw near to you.
James 4:8 (NIV)

Power Points for Daily Living: Meditation Moments

Power Points for Daily Living: Meditation Moments

DAY 12
Change is Growth!

He who rejects change is the architect of decay. The only human institution which rejects progress is the cemetery.
Harold Wilson

Power Points for Daily Living: Meditation Moments

Power Points for Daily Living: Meditation Moments

DAY 13
How's your perspective?

Just because everything is different doesn't mean anything has changed.
Irene Peter

Power Points for Daily Living: Meditation Moments

DAY 14
How's your prospective?

The greatest inventions and accomplishments began as the flicker of an idea. This tiny flame was then fueled by desire and faith. Watch out for those tiny little ideas. You have the potential to turn them into great things.
Steve Brunkhorst

Power Points for Daily Living: Meditation Moments

Power Points for Daily Living: Meditation Moments

DAY 15
Turn the other way!

A man who wants to lead the orchestra must turn his back on the crowd.
Max Lucado

Power Points for Daily Living: Meditation Moments

Power Points for Daily Living: Meditation Moments

DAY 16
Take the Risk!

You cannot climb a mountain if you will not risk a fall.
Rick Beneteau

Power Points for Daily Living: Meditation Moments

Power Points for Daily Living: Meditation Moments

DAY 17
It's Possible!

Ordinary people believe only in the possible. Extraordinary people visualize not what is possible or probable, but rather what is impossible. And by visualizing the impossible, they begin to see it as possible.
Cherie Carter-Scott

Power Points for Daily Living: Meditation Moments

Power Points for Daily Living: Meditation Moments

DAY 18
A Mouth Full!

Learn to swallow, or you will chock!
Joseph J. Grant

Power Points for Daily Living: Meditation Moments

Power Points for Daily Living: Meditation Moments

DAY 19
Spit it out!

Learn what to swallow or you will die; Poison kills!
Lillie M. Grant

Power Points for Daily Living: Meditation Moments

Power Points for Daily Living: Meditation Moments

DAY 20
The little things

Be faithful in small things because it is in them that your strength lies.
Mother Teresa

Power Points for Daily Living: Meditation Moments

Power Points for Daily Living: Meditation Moments

DAY 21
Get Up!

If you have made mistakes, there is always another chance for you. You may have a fresh start any moment you choose, for this thing we call 'failure' is not the falling down, but the staying down.
Mary Pickford

Power Points for Daily Living: Meditation Moments

Power Points for Daily Living: Meditation Moments

DAY 22
Just Believe!

Faith consists in believing when it is beyond the power of reason to believe.
Voltaire

Power Points for Daily Living: Meditation Moments

Power Points for Daily Living: Meditation Moments

DAY 23
Handle it!

*Experience is not what happens to you;
it is what you do with what happens to you.*
Aldous Huxley

Power Points for Daily Living: Meditation Moments

Power Points for Daily Living: Meditation Moments

DAY 24
Don't let go!

*When you feel like giving up,
remember why you held on for so long in the first place.*
unknown

Power Points for Daily Living: Meditation Moments

Power Points for Daily Living: Meditation Moments

DAY 25
Go Crazy!

I don't like myself, I'm crazy about myself.
Mae West

Power Points for Daily Living: Meditation Moments

Power Points for Daily Living: Meditation Moments

DAY 26
What do you believe?

You don't become what you want; you become what you believe.
Oprah Winfrey

Power Points for Daily Living: Meditation Moments

Power Points for Daily Living: Meditation Moments

DAY 27
Let it go!

Sometimes you've got to let everything go—purge yourself... If you are unhappy with anything... whatever is bringing you down, get rid of it. Because you'll find that when you're free, your true creativity, your true self comes out.
Tina Turner

Power Points for Daily Living: Meditation Moments

Power Points for Daily Living: Meditation Moments

DAY 28
Undefeated!

You may encounter many defeats, but you must not be defeated. In fact, it may be necessary to encounter the defeats, so you can know who you are, what you can rise from, how you can still come out of it.
Maya Angelou

Power Points for Daily Living: Meditation Moments

Day 29
Give it a try!

I really don't think life is about the I-could-have-beens. Life is only about the I-tried-to-do. I don't mind the failure but I can't imagine that I'd forgive myself if I didn't try.
Nikki Giovanni

Power Points for Daily Living: Meditation Moments

Power Points for Daily Living: Meditation Moments

DAY 30
The Power Within!

Never underestimate the power of dreams and the influence of the human spirit. We are all the same in this notion: The potential for greatness lives within each of us.
Wilma Rudolph

Power Points for Daily Living: Meditation Moments

www.ingramcontent.com/pod-product-compliance
Lightning Source LLC
Chambersburg PA
CBHW050603300426
44112CB00013B/2043